Writing
Rules!

A Mysterious Student Handbook by
Lilly Maytree

Summers Island Press
Thorne Bay, Alaska

Summers Island Press
P.O. Box 19293
Thorne Bay, AK 99919

Website: www.SummersIslandPress.com

 Summers Island Press is an imprint of the Wilderness School Institute, a non-profit educational organization that offers outdoor youth activities in wilderness settings, including training in wilderness skills and nature studies, as well as the publication of curriculum on related subjects, through the Wilderness School Press, and their children's imprint Summers Island Press.

/Hardback Edition

Lilly Maytree's Mysterious Student Handbooks are a shortcuts to understanding the basic rules of a particular subject in a way that will be valuable in the future. What's so mysterious about it? This unusual method of learning triggers the subconscious into learning other subjects at the same time you are busy learning this one.

Students of any age can enjoy the pleasures of mastering these essential skills that will help them confidently face assignments in other subject areas, as well.

Nothing adds more to the enjoyment of learning as much as knowing your way around the fundamentals that are common to every educational field. All levels of reading, writing, math, and science will be easier for any student who first understands the basics.

*To all those who ever wished it could
be easier than it looks... it can!*

"Wisdom is the most important thing."

King Solomon

Contents

1

Introduction

A Word About Words...

Words can take you places. You can learn things from them. Sometimes, they can even be little vehicles that actually transport feelings from one person to another. Words are the highest form of communication there is. Communicating to each other with words is what separates humans from animals.

Much of what we learn comes through the experience of others that we discover by reading books. To be able to express yourself by writing in a way that will help others understand you better is a skill that is easy to learn. One that will not only be helpful to you in school but for the rest of your life, too.

Writing well comes from learning basic rules and then practicing them. You can also learn what good writing is by reading a lot. But the best way to become a good writer is by doing both. If you are reading this, you're old enough to know that not all writing is interesting. In fact, a lot of things you have to read are pretty boring. Do you know why? Let's take a closer look and find out...

2

The Sentence

A sentence is a group of words that expresses a complete thought.

Sentences are the most common way ideas are communicated from one person's brain to another. The best way to express the exact meaning of what you are thinking is by using a complete sentence.

For instance, you wouldn't just say, *"Next to the bookcase,"* to someone and have them understand exactly what you mean. On the other hand, *"The shoe you are missing is next to the bookcase,"* gets the point across. Of course, if you noticed your sister hobbling around on one shoe while she searched the living room, *"Next to the bookcase,"* might be enough said right then.

People who know each other well—especially families —often talk to each other in pieces of sentences that are called **fragments**. In writing, this is not enough. You will see a sentence fragment once in a while, but only when it is surrounded by information that makes its meaning perfectly clear, and usually just for emphasis.

Computers do not understand this. Programs that check spelling and grammar will always point out a sentence fragment as something that should be changed. That's because computers do not think: they simply gather and give out information. The truth is, there are certain times in writing when a fragment IS acceptable.

Kinds of Sentences

All sentences begin with a capital letter and end with a punctuation mark.

The Declarative Sentence

The most common kind is one that simply makes a statement. This is called a declarative sentence (comes from the word declare, which means to state something). *"Blue is a pretty color,"* is a declarative sentence. You might agree with it and you might not. It probably will not cause a surge of any feelings inside you. On the other hand, *"After her twelfth birthday, Mystery Girl was in a good mood whenever she wore blue,"* makes a person curious.

Not just about who "Mystery Girl" might be, but why the color blue had such an effect on her. You might even wonder what happened on her twelfth birthday to make her feel this way. If there are more sentences following which promise to explain these things, a reader will want to read on.

Both of these sentences are correct sentences. Both of them are declarative. Only the second one brings certain thoughts to your mind and then propels you forward. It causes you to think or wonder about something. In other words, it makes a better connection with your brain. Sort of like someone throwing you a ball.

The Interrogative Sentence

This kind of sentence asks a question and always ends with a question mark. If you are wondering how you will ever remember a word as long as interrogative, just think of the word interrogate, which means to question someone.

Even though it has a difficult name, it is one of the easiest kinds of sentences to recognize. *"Did you find what you were looking for?"* is an interrogative sentence. So is, *"What time is it?"* or *"Do you think she knew she was being followed?"*

Interrogative sentences make good links for paragraphs, because they naturally cause a reader to want to see the answer and read on.

The Exclamatory Sentence

This kind of sentence expresses strong feeling, or emotion, and always has an exclamation point at the end. In writing, the exclamation point also shows us when someone is yelling, such as the sentence, *"Turn the radio down!"*

Even though an exclamatory sentence is easy to identify, they can be a little tricky when you try to write one. That's because not every place you could put an exclamation point should have one. Too many exclamations in your writing can actually make it less exciting if you "give the signal" for excitement and then don't follow through with anything exciting.

For example, *"Mother invited the neighbor to dinner!"* would not seem very exciting to most people. In fact, they might even think it was a little silly or over dramatic and stop reading.

On the other hand, if you wrote, *"Mother invited an alien to dinner!"*... that little change in the sentence would bring to mind all sorts of problems that might happen. The reader would simply have to read on just to find out.

The Imperative Sentence

This is a sentence that commands. A good way to think of an imperative sentence is to think of the word *imperial*. This makes us think of kings, who have the authority to command. You can also think of the word *important*: because most commands that are given to us are important.

"*Follow the yellow brick road,*" is an imperative sentence. Without it, Dorothy could never have found her way to the Emerald City. "*Get out of the way!*" is also an imperative sentence, even though it has an exclamation point at the end. Why? Because while the exclamation point still expresses more excitement or intense feeling than an ordinary sentence, it is—more importantly—a command to do something.

There are more kinds of sentences and there are many different books and web sites available where you can learn more about them if you are interested. But the four different kinds we have looked at are the most common.

Understanding the difference between them can make anything you write easier for others to understand. If you never learn anything else about sentences, this information will get you by, whether you are working on a class assignment or a letter to a friend. Because now you know the basics.

Here is an example of the same sentence written in each of the four basic ways:

The boy got out of the burning building.
(declarative sentence)

Did the boy get out of the burning building?
(interrogatory sentence)

Thank heaven, that boy got out of the building!
(exclamatory sentence)

Boy, get out of the building!
(imperative sentence)

Something You Should Know...

The most important goal in writing anything is to make sure your words are interesting enough to keep readers reading.

3

The Paragraph

A paragraph links several sentences together that focus on the same topic; to amplify, explain, or defend that topic.

A paragraph may be one word long or a thousand words long. If the point of the paragraph has been made, then it is long enough. We have much shorter paragraphs today than a hundred years ago.

That's probably because TV and movies have made it less necessary to describe everything so thoroughly. For example, the phrase tropical island is enough to help you picture it in your mind without having to explain that there is a sandy beach, palm trees, and maybe a volcano. Most of us have already seen such places many times on TV. We also have busier lifestyles these days, and a lot of readers don't enjoy long explanations. They would rather have action. Or at least have things get right to the point.

What's The Point?

Every paragraph has a point to make, and this point is known as the **topic sentence**. It almost always comes first, but occasionally last, if the paragraph is made up of details that require a **summary**. Such as:

Dinner was still cooking on the stove. Purse and keys sat on a shelf next to the coat rack. In the living room, a vase of flowers lay broken on the floor and even one of the chairs was tipped over. *Every clue in the house pointed to a kidnapping.*

Something You Should Know...

Reading only the first sentence of every paragraph is a fast way to "skim" the most important facts from a long chapter in a textbook. It is also a good way to research the answers to questions when you don't know exactly where to find them.

For the most part, you will find the topic sentence at the beginning. It is the one that states or summarizes the theme of the paragraph. It is what the rest of the paragraph is going to be about.

Which brings us to the point that all the sentences in a paragraph are related. When you write a paragraph, you should concentrate on one main idea. If there is a sentence in your paragraph that changes the subject... it doesn't belong there.

You should not include things that don't continue or describe your central thought. If it is something important that you don't want to leave out, you can say in another paragraph.

Use Your Thumb

All paragraphs need to be indented to let readers know a new paragraph is starting. If you are writing by hand, the old fashioned rule of putting your thumb on the line and starting the first sentence right after it still works best. The rest of the sentences are contained within the margins. If you are using a keyboard, pressing the spacebar five times, does the same thing.

The "tab" key will also work to indent, but tabs are changeable, so you have to make sure the first setting is for a first line indent of five spaces. Occasionally, a single-spaced business letter, ebook, or email, will divide paragraphs by putting a blank line space between them without using any first line indents. But for most formal writing, such as reports or class assignments, indenting the first line of paragraphs is correct.

Make It Clear

Writing clearly—or being specific—is what separates good paragraph writing from bad. It is better to say, *"The teacher criticized our mistakes in front of the class, and* sent students to stand outside for the smallest reasons," than to say, *"The teacher was mean."*

That's because people usually feel stronger about their own opinions than somebody else's. If you can write in such a way that your readers will "see" things the way you do, they will come to the same conclusion. Your writing will be stronger because you have caused them to respond to something in their own way.

It is also better to describe someone's eyes, ears, nose, and skin than to simply say he was ugly or handsome. Look at the following two examples:

The man puffed when he breathed, like a giant bullfrog. The boy sat in the seat across from him and watched the mustache beneath a big red nose quiver with every breath.

The large man who sat down across from the boy was tired out.

Do you see how one makes you imagine a picture, and the other doesn't? Showing specific things about people, places, or feelings, helps readers imagine better pictures.
It helps them "see" what you mean more clearly.

Where Does It Go?

Not many paragraphs stand by themselves, except maybe in advertising or in a brief description of things under a picture. Most of them are grouped together to either tell a story or explain information on a particular subject.

In most assignments, three to four paragraphs is enough to answer questions, give an opinion, or write a short essay. A few pages is the average for a short story or report. On the other hand, you could fill an entire notebook by the end of the year with thoughts you put down on paper at the rate of a page a day.

At the same time, a collection of perfect paragraphs does not always guarantee a perfect assignment. They all have to be put in the best possible order...

And there's a trick to that.

Something You Should Know...

Paragraphs link sentences and are themselves linked to one another.

4

The Links

Transitional words and phrases are the best way to link sentences and paragraphs together so they will read smoothly.

While a paragraph has a point to make and includes enough sentences to show, prove, or give good reasons for that point, it still needs something else. It needs links and bridges that connect each one together in a logical way. Good writing is rather like a train that needs a smooth track to run on and a coupling for each car. Without those it can't take you anywhere.

Like a train ride, the main reason for getting on is to go somewhere. And just as a traveler by rail hopes there won't be any delays or breakdowns along the way, readers are no different. They would especially like to see something exciting during their travels. If the trip is too long, or there is too much of the same scenery, it gets boring.

Nobody likes boring.

It is even more unpleasant to get lost. Which happens in writing when things get confusing, or change subjects too fast, or never make any point at all. The best way to avoid these things is to know where you are headed before you even start out.

Lining Things Up

Just as it helps to know your destination, or maybe even have a map to follow as you begin a trip, it is a good idea to have an **outline** of your ideas before you actually start writing your paragraphs. There are many different kinds of outlines.

They can be a few words jotted down on a piece of notepaper, several pages of **research data** organized under letters and **Roman numerals**, or anything in between. You only need as much as it takes to know where you are going.

Let's say you are running for president of a bird watching club, and have been asked to write a paragraph about yourself for the next bulletin. With only three or four sentences to work with there would not be enough space to tell your entire life story.

But if you had earned a wildlife merit badge from a scouting program, achieved amateur naturalist status with your lifetime bird list, or traveled to an African game reserve to study the ostrich; these are the things bird watchers would want to know about. Being the youngest out of a family of six, or having been voted the most valuable player in a recent volleyball tournament would not be **relevant**.

An outline helps you decide what is important to include in your paragraphs and reminds you to stay on track with your subject. So, an outline for the above example might look like this:

Merit badge

Amateur naturalist

African trip

Joke about birds

But just as road maps are simply a tool to help you decide what choices are available for you to take, and there is no law that you have to follow them, you can change your mind about outlines, too. You can rearrange things any way you want. If you realized your paragraph was going to be too long if you included all those things, you might change your outline to look something like this:

Merit badge

Amateur naturalist

African trip

~~Joke about birds~~

But what if you were writing a story about birds for an English assignment, and it had to be five pages long? Then an outline like the following would be more helpful:

I. Eric Peabody

   A. President of bird club

   B. Eagle Scout

   C. Son of Ambassador to Africa

II. Kidnapped

A. While visiting game reserve

B. Escapes using scout survival skills

C. Discovers who is poaching ostriches from the reserve

III. Becomes famous

A. Gets interviewed on the nightly news

B. Is adopted into a native tribe

C. Gets featured in *National Geographic Kids World*

Not only would this outline keep you on track with your story, you could also use it to organize any research information you might need to look up. Such as writing some facts about the area your story will take place under "Son of Ambassador to Africa," or information on the habits of the ostrich under "Discovers who is poaching ostriches from the reserve." You might even list the most important survival skills Eric uses to escape from his captors.

Using an outline makes the actual writing easier. In fact, the more detailed you get with your outline, the less time you will spend wondering what to write next, or what you should do first. On the other hand, you can even keep an outline all in your head for shorter, simpler projects.

No matter how you use them, outlines are a tool to help you keep from getting "lost" along the way throughout your writing project. Just like a map.

Hooking It All Together

You can have the best ideas and great information, but if you don't put things in the right order so that they read smooth and logical, people will have a hard time understanding what you want to say.

To avoid this, it is important to use some **universal** language in your writing. These are the words and phrases that everyone understands. They are like traffic signals: pretty self-explanatory no matter what language you speak. And they do the same thing.

This universal language is made up of words like **because, however, then again, after that, whenever, this, in the same way, next**, and many more. Sometimes, simply repeating a word or phrase from a preceding sentence or paragraph is enough of a signal to "carry" the reader along.

These are called **transition** words and phrases, because they indicate that something else related to the subject is coming, and prompt a reader to keep reading. Look at the following example...

Without transitions:

Eric opened one eye. Where had everybody gone? There was no time to think about that. If ever there was a chance to escape, this was it. Who knew how long it would last? He would sneak off so quietly nobody would notice he was missing. He would open the ostrich pens, first. They would just be rounded up, again. Some might get away.

While they were making their escape, Eric would be making his, too. If that old tracker had been right about a full moon tonight, he could get as far as the river by morning. He would really be on his own.

With transitions:

Eric opened one eye. Where had everybody gone? **But** there was no time to think about that, **now**. If ever there was a chance to escape, this was it. **Besides**, who knew how long it would last? **Maybe** he could sneak off so quietly nobody would notice he was missing. **Of course**, he would open the ostrich pens, first. They would probably **just** be rounded up, again, but some might get away.

And while those giant birds were making their escape, Eric would be making his, too. If that old tracker had been right about a full moon tonight, he **might even** get as far as the river by morning. **Then** he would really be on his own.

Visual Signals

Another way to keep your writing smooth and to help readers see things exactly the way you do, is through punctuation. Like traffic signals, punctuation marks tell a reader when to stop (a period), slow down (a comma), or speed up (an exclamation mark).

Three dots in a row (...also known as an *ellipsis*) means that there have either been words left out, that someone didn't finish what they were saying, or that the rest is following in another sentence or paragraph.

Sometimes, simply adding a blank line above and beneath a sentence or paragraph will give it extra emphasis. Such as when you are quoting something. In the help section at the end of this booklet, you will find a more extensive list of punctuation marks and how to use them, along with a list of steps on how to **edit** your own writing for a **final draft**.

These things will help you make sure that what you write is the very best you can do, with no overlooked mistakes, or boring writing. It is a good idea to look over these lists each time you finish a writing assignment, just to make sure you have remembered all the rules.

Is That All?

Of course not. If you are really interested in writing well, you can learn a lot more from studying grammar, advanced writing techniques, and reading good literature. You can search out more information on the web, or in libraries. You can even look through a few English textbooks and get some practice in the areas you are most interested in.

But if you never do any of the above things, what we have talked about here will help you write well enough to perform most class assignments. And it will keep helping you communicate your thoughts better whenever yo have to write them down. Because as long as you stick to these simple basics... your **writing rules!**

5
Quick Helps

Following are two lists you can refer back to that will help you check any writing assignment before turning it in.

Punctuation

Period [.]

1. Use a period to show the end of a sentence.

Eric Peabody is different than most kids.

Not many people are as resourceful as he is.

2. Use period after certain abbreviations.

Washington **D.C.** is the city where the president lives.

Dr. Livingston spent many years in Africa.

The famous Sherlock Holmes lived at 221B Baker **St.** in London.

It is 4:00 **p.m.** in the Congo right now.

Question Mark [?]

Use a question mark at the end of a sentence to show a direct question.

How many birds do you see**?**

NOTE: do not use a question mark for indirect questions. Following is a sample of an indirect

question:

> The kidnapper didn't take Eric's map. Do not ask me why.

Exclamation Mark [!]

Use an exclamation mark at the end of a sentence to show surprise or excitement.

> Watch out for that ostrich!
>
> We were lost!

Comma[,]

1. Use a comma to show a pause in a sentence.

> Therefore, the compass needle will always point north.

2. Use a comma with quotation marks to show what someone has said directly.

> "I can climb any mountain," she said, "but I have to have the right equipment."

3. Use commas for listing three or more different things.

> A flashlight, compass, and matches are three things every camper needs.

4. Use commas around phrases that add extra

information to a sentence.

> Davy Crockett, who was the last man to die at the Alamo, was best known for being honest and brave.

Apostrophe [']

1. Use and apostrophe to show ownership of something.

> This is Eric's handwriting.

> These are the scientist's things. (things that belong to the scientist)

Note: For nouns in plural form, put the apostrophe at the end of the noun.

> These are the scientists' things. (things that belong to the scientists)

2. Use an apostrophe to show letters that have been left out of a word.

> I don't know how to operate it.

Quotation Marks ["]

Use quotation marks to show what someone has said directly.

> The police officer said, "We will catch the kidnappers."

"Not one step further," he said, "or I'll shoot"

Colon [:]

1. Use a colon to introduce a list of things.

There are three things a first aid worker must take care of immediately: bleeding, breathing, and poisoning.

2. Use a colon to introduce a long quotation.

The Ambassador said: "We will work together. We will use all our resources. We will bring Eric Peabody home."

Semicolon[;]

1. Us a semicolon to join related sentences together.

The farmer's market is very popular; people from all over town come every Saturday.

2. Use a semicolon in lists that already have commas.

The three busiest airports in the United States are in Seattle, Washington; Newark, New Jersey; and Denver, Colorado.

Dash [-]

1. Use a dash before a phrase that summarizes the idea of a sentence.

>Tired, sunburned, and sandy—these are the things you feel most after a day at the beach.

2. Use a dash before and after a phrase or list that adds extra information in the middle of a sentence.

>The puppies—Spotty, Lucky, and Pokey—all escaped through the hole in the fence.

>Most of the students in her class—but not all—made it onto the honor roll.

3. Use a dash to show that someone has been interrupted when speaking.

>The boy said, "I was only trying to—" but the principal shuffled him into the office before we could hear the explanation.

Hyphen [-]

1. Use a hyphen to join two words that form one idea together.

>sour-tasting

>earth-shaking

2. Use a hyphen to join prefixes to words.

Anti-American

non-profit

3. Use a hyphen when writing compound numbers.

three-quarters

twenty-one

Revising

1. Write in the active voice:

Faulty: In each face the sadness is shown.

Better: Each face shows the sadness.

2. Use personal pronouns (I, we, our) **when they are appropriate and especially when they clarify your text:**

Faulty: It has been found in studies that people who take vitamins are healthier.

Better: In our studies, we found that people who take vitamins are healthier.

3. Write sentences that have people doing things:

Faulty: It was decided that Eric Peabody be elected for president of the bird club.

Better: We elected Eric Peabody for president of our bird club.

4. Substitute descriptive verbs for vague verbs:

Faulty: He went back to school with his discovery.

Better: He ran back to school with his discovery.

5. Substitute familiar for unfamiliar words:

> *Faulty:* Everyone should be cognizant of the dangers of global warming.

> *Better:* Everyone should be aware of the dangers of global warming.

6. Avoid overused expressions

> *Faulty:* The instructions have to be crystal clear to avoid slip-shod work.

> *Better:* The instructions have to be very clear to avoid sloppy work.

7. Cut unnecessary words:

> *Faulty:* After a wait of one or two minutes, the elevator will return.

> *Better:* After one or two minutes, the elevator will return.

8. Be precise:

> *Faulty:* The temperature was really high outside.

> *Better:* The temperature was a hundred and ten degrees outside.

Glossary

Here are definitions for the most important bold-faced words and terms used in this booklet.

D

Declarative sentence

The kind of sentence that makes a statement or "declares" something

E

Edit

To prepare by correcting, revising, or adapting

Essay

A short literary composition on a single subject, usually presenting the personal view of the author

Emphasis

Importance given to a syllable, word, or words, through punctuation, or printing in italic type

Exclamation point

A punctuation mark (!) used after an abrupt and emphatic statement, or after a command to indicate strong feeling, or high volume

Exclamatory sentence

A sentence that ends with an exclamation point

F

Final draft

The last and best copy of your writing after all corrections and revisions

Fragments

An incomplete or isolated portion; a small part broken off , or detached

I

Imperative sentence

A sentence that requests or demands that an action be performed

Interrogatory sentence

A sentence that asks a question

O

Outline

A general description covering the main points of a subject

or

A summary of a written work or speech, usually analyzed in headings and subheadings

P

Punctuation mark

The marks used to clarify meaning by indicating separation of words into sentences and phrases

R

Relevant

Having a bearing on or connection with the matter at hand

Roman numerals

Any of the numerical symbols formed with the Roman letters I,V, X, L, C, D, and M, representing the numbers 1, 5, 10, 50, 100, and 1000, used by the ancient Romans, and still used today in certain formal contexts.

Research data

Factual information, especially information organized for analysis, used to reason or make decisions

S

Specific

Exact, definite

Summary

A presentation of the substance of a body of material in a condensed form or by reducing it to it's main points

T

Theme

A central idea in a piece of writing or other work of art

Topic sentence

The sentence within a paragraph that states the main thought, often placed at the beginning

Transitional

A word, phrase, sentence, or series of sentences connecting one part of a discourse to another

U

Universal

Of, relating to, extending to, or affecting the entire world, or all within the world; worldwide

Thank you for reading this book. If you found it helpful, tell someone! At Summers Island Press—the home of mysteriously different books for children—you can find fiction and nonfiction for all ages. It is also the home of Wilderness Kids Club, where there is always something better to do.

Summers Island Press, along with their adult imprint Lightsmith Publishers, is a division of the Wilderness School Institute, a non-profit educational organization based in Thorne Bay, Alaska. You can find out more by visiting:

www.SummersIslandPress.com

About Lilly Maytree

Lilly Maytree is a novelist who spent many years learning about words so that you wouldn't have to. She is also good at finding adventures. And it should be pointed out that she is related to Cousin Summers (the Mysterious), but you would have to get to know her better before she would tell you anything about that. However, if you would like to try, she can always be found over at:

www.LillyMaytree.com

If she isn't there, try, again... she always comes back sooner, or later. She would like to hear from you!

Other books by
Lilly Maytree

Novels:

Gold Trap

The Pandora Box

The Stella Madison Capers:

Home Before Dark

A Thief In The House

Sea Trials

The Pushover Plot

Lost In The Wilderness

The Last Resort

Voyage of the Dreadnaught

For Writers:

Unspoken Rules

For Parents:

Behave Yourself!
Teaching children to dicipline themselves.

www.ingramcontent.com/pod-product-compliance
Lightning Source LLC
Chambersburg PA
CBHW051858090426
42811CB00003B/376

MOUNT VERNON

HAS A STORY TO TELL

Mount Vernon

Hampton Publishing House, LLC
P.O. Box 29001
Columbus, OH 43229

2

ISBN 978-0-9828745-9-2

Printed in the United States of America

A Historical Place in Columbus, Ohio

MOUNT VERNON AVENUE

Written by Melica Niccole
Illustrated by Viviana Moyano

Unity, socialization, and a sense of community

Hampton Publishing House, LLC

Written by
Melica Niccole

Illustrated by
Viviana Moyano

Edited By
Monae Jones

This book is dedicated to
Annie B. and Daisy P. Grandmother and mother,
thank you. Thank you for allowing me to experience
Mount Vernon through your stories and through
special events.

I love you both.

Rest in peace, Grandma
I miss you.

I would also like to dedicate this book to known and
unknown artists who captured life in their pictures
and illustrations about Mount Vernon and
neighboring districts.

Special Acknowledgement

Thanking all of those who provided stories about their experiences on Mount Vernon. Some of your stories were taken into consideration when developing this book.

Table of Contents

Rodney Hears the sounds of the neighborhood

I hear the streets coming to life as people begin to pound the concrete and socialize. Rodney, down the way, comes outside. He brings his saxophone and begins to play. The beautiful sounds from his instrument travels up and down Mount Vernon Avenue. The scene fades out and another scene fades in. The scene shown is of a small boy being prepped on how to play the saxophone because his mother said so. A beautiful sound is entering the ears of a mother whose son may not even know the song that blares from his instrument.

He practices day and night. His childhood is being robbed from him like a man robbed of his sight. His discomfort comes from his many saxophone lessons that he respectfully dreads. He asks his mother, "Mama, why do I have to play this instrument day after day? I have no time to play with my friends. I just want to have fun." The mother answers with authority, "Because unlike your friends, you have a mother that cares for you. I don't want to see you running around these streets, learning the street life, or sitting on the corner, on a stoop, laughing your whole life away. You are better than these streets. You are better than the life that leads down the wrong path. You, my son, were made for greatness."

Rodney plays his saxophone on Mount Vernon Avenue, unleashing the story of his childhood through his beautiful music. Memories of his mother and what she taught him exerts itself in the tunes he blows from his golden instrument. Beautiful sounds and beautiful people grace Mount Vernon Avenue. Rodney begins to remember how Mount Vernon was once graced with beautiful shades of people from all walks of life, all shapes, sizes, and shades. He remembers people putting on their finest outfits to dance and have fun at The Cameo and The Olympia. He also remembers historic events like the Coming Home and when Robert Kennedy (John F. Kennedy's brother) ran for president and graced the streets of Mount Vernon.

There is so much rich history in that area that Rodney did not want to forget about the past. He did not want to forget about the unity of people that brought forth a culture of traditions. Most of all, he did not want to forget about Mount Vernon and what it still means to him. To Rodney, Mount Vernon Avenue was a place of self-identification. It allowed a group of people to come together and unite because of the music, art, food, and much more. Rodney must give respect, where respect is due. He must give respect to Mount Vernon Avenue for making him

the man that he is today.

Annie B's Cameo Days

A beautiful, fair-skinned woman makes her way down Mount Vernon Avenue. She is wearing a black fur coat with a hat that matches it. She is approximately 4 feet and 2 inches tall; however, her black high heel shoes put a couple more inches on her. She continues her graceful stride down the street, making every movement more pronounced.

The men stop and stare. It seems that they recognize beauty when they see it. The men even watch her stop, fix her pantyhose, and then keep with the same pace she was walking before she had stopped. If there is one thing Annie has, it is grace.

As she continues her stride down Mount Vernon Avenue, she begins to think about all the wonderful fun she is going to have at The Cameo.

The Cameo is the "What's Happening" place of Columbus, Ohio. It is the place where everyone wants to go and if you are not old enough to be there, it is the place that you dream about going.

Annie entered the building and met up with the sisters of Mount Vernon. The group embraces each other as if they have not seen each other in years. It has only been a day or so since their last social event.

The music is blaring as a live jazz band plays a multitude of songs that forces people to do several well-known dances: The Lindy Hop, The Collegiate Shag, Heel Shag, Big Apple, and Black Bottom. A handsome dark-skinned gentleman makes his way over to Annie's side. Expressions of familiarity come across their faces, as he pulls her onto the dance floor. They sway back and forth across the dance floor, jumping and hopping to the sounds of Martha

Reeves and the Vandellas. It is one of those moments to live and die for. It is a moment where everyone stops to watch two rhythmically inclined individuals make their mark on life.

Another mark is made immediately following the first one. It is a mark that leaves everyone stunned and astounded at the behavior of a certain individual. The individual is Annie's husband, Isaac. He walks into The Cameo, right past the cashier. He has a very stern walk with only one thing on his mind: his wife. Shocked at his wife dancing with another fellow, he grabs her arm in mid-motion and escorts her to the door. He says nothing as he grabs her coat off the coat rack and keeps with his same stride. Annie, soul mate of Isaac, knows better than to object to her husband's lovingly method to bring her home.

As Annie looks into her husband's eyes in their bedroom, she begins to remember. She remembers the life they once had in Marianna, Arkansas. She remembers attending college in Little Rock, Arkansas. She even remembers going to a cotton field to pick cotton for money. Isaac is the love of her life. Why else would she let him take her from her home in Arkansas and move to Columbus, Ohio for a better opportunity?

The thing about Annie is that she isn't your typical stay-at-home type of wife. She is the type who likes to have fun while she still has a chance to have it. Her husband, on the other hand, would prefer to spend a nice, quiet evening at home with his family, which includes Annie.

Ray Loves the Weekends on Mount Vernon

Ray jumps up from his bed without even thinking. "I'm late," he yells as he makes his way to the bathroom. It is exactly 10:15 AM. The door slams [Thump]. The sound of pounding water from the shower can be heard. Ray strolls out of the bathroom, 20 minutes later with a towel wrapped around his waist.

"Damn that boy looks good," he says as he passes himself in the mirror.

Ray quickly throws on a nice pair of dress slacks, a silk shirt, and a pair of polished Howard and Foster's from Rosenberg Shoes. In these times, clothes speak a lot about a person's character. Ray's clothes are definitely speaking to him, and they are saying, "Boy, you sure look good."

16

Ray runs outside, just in time to catch the weekly parades on Mount Vernon Avenue. He looks forward to these parades. It is a way that people in the neighborhood can express themselves in an artistic manner. The greatest part about the parades is that they happen every weekend at the same time and place.

Still amazed at what has just taken place, Ray passes Lee's Style Shop on his way to Woolworth's in a trance. Suddenly, he notices the long line of men in the shop wearing gold and sharkskin suits. A thought enters Ray's mind, "Man, I can dig that." This is his reaction to a man standing in front of Lee's with a white suit, matching hat, and a flock of women surrounding him.

After taking in all the wonderful sights, Ray finally makes it to Woolworths. He just can't wait to sink his teeth into the block of peanut butter and chocolate that has been waiting for him. Well, almost sink. The block candy is always so thick and hard that it must be broken into pieces just to eat it. Ray slid right up to the counter like a garden snake. "Two pieces of peanut butter chocolate, please," he says smiling. "That will be ten cents." He pulled a dime from his pocket and handed it over to the store clerk.

With thoughts of peanut butter and chocolate on the brain, Ray walks hastily past a group of children. All of a sudden, he hears someone shout, "Uh, I'm telling Mama." He looks up to see his baby sister, Nettie, right in front of him with her hand stuck out. "I won't tell if you give me a piece." His first thoughts are, "What type of power does Netti have to try and get one over on me? This is my candy. Why should I have to share?" Ray gives his little sister a piece of candy by nearly throwing it right at her. He decides to be kind because he is unable to justify his food choices to his parents, especially right before dinner.

Before dinner, Ray stands on his front stoop to wait for his girlfriend's parents to drop her off. His girlfriend's name is Eva Mae. Eva Mae is a beautiful, short, dark-skinned girl with long, jet black hair. Eva Mae's family is from the Mount Vernon area; however, they had recently became residents of Pennsylvania over the past two months. Every so often, the family would drive approximately three hours so Ray and Eva Mae could visit each other.

After having a long conversation with his mother, Ray decides that he will take Eva Mae to dinner at the Chesapeake. The food at the Chesapeake is amazing. The menu includes everything from succulent barbeque chicken to scrumptious macaroni salad. Ray thought it would be

19

a wonderful change from his mother always having to cook and them spending time with his family. It was nothing against his family; he just wanted Eva Mae all to himself.

Tonight, Ray is on a roll. He surprises the love of his life with movie tickets to the Pythonian Theater. The Pythonian is a great theater. It is a place where the couple can enjoy their movie upstairs and then dance the night away downstairs. Eva Mae is surprised and gives Ray a long-awaited kiss he has been anticipating since they made plans to spend the night alone.

Daisy meets Robert Kennedy

A beautiful, dark-skinned woman of five foot stature walks down 17th Avenue. 17th Avenue is the street in which a lot of African-Americans reside and is approximately two streets over from Mount Vernon Avenue. It is also the same street where Daisy dwells.

Daisy is around twenty years old. She doesn't have any children; however, she often daydreams about falling in love and having three or four kids. What more could this former graduate of East High want besides a husband and kids? Well, there is a lot more that she wants. She also thinks about becoming a famous writer, like Langston Hughes, Maya Angelou, and Richard Wright.

Great news of Robert Kennedy campaigning in Columbus, Ohio spreads around the neighborhood. Daisy is even more excited to hear that he will be visiting the Mount Vernon area. Daisy, native of Mobile, Alabama, never dreamt of the day that she would meet a nationally recognized figure.

Daisy wears a summery dress, displaying flowers and the beautiful colors of green, cream, and pink. This is a very historic moment that she has to be a part of. Daisy decides to attend the event with two of her best friends from high school. The spectators become overly excited as a float carrying Mr. Kennedy comes down Mount Vernon. It is amazing to see the large crowds of people trying to touch and shake his hand. Daisy is not sure whether her friends got an opportunity to shake Mr. Kennedy's hand; however, she extends her hand and accepts his hand in exchange for hers. Daisy thinks

to herself, "Oh, what a glorious day!"

Mount Vernon in the eyes of Melica

Ten students sit in a classroom. There is a potential for more students to attend the program; however, it is too nice outside to keep track of who and who is not here. It is a beautiful Saturday morning with a great chance of being eighty degrees by noon. Melica focuses on being able to enjoy the beautiful weather, instead of the tedious multiplication drills that so enthusiastically come from the instructor's mouth. Focusing is not a strong suite for Melica; however, with the right rewards, anything is possible.

You must understand that Melica's aunt, Sadie keeps her two nieces engaged in various activities that would teach them to be law-abiding citizens and encourage hard work. This time, Sadie, registered her kids and nieces into a tutoring program that would spark their growth and development. There will be no more ballet or selling Girl Scout cookies for these four. Sadie has bigger dreams for her family and knows that life is not just about dancing, functioning in social groups, and the artistic side of things. Life is about understanding, communication553, and of course, math.

Melica sits in the classroom, ready for fun, not realizing the benefits that the small tutoring session on Mount Vernon Avenue will have on her future. She does not realize that math plays a big role in various daily activities, such as counting, shopping, budgeting, and getting paid. If only all this information could mean something to her now, as it would in the future, she would know just what to do with it. The scene fades out and another scene fades in. A young woman sits in a well-lit room, calculating her budget for the New Year. She thinks about various expenses she has, such as rent, electricity, car insurance, and much more. This woman must pay homage to the road she has traveled to get to where she is today. She must revisit those multiplication lessons on Mount Vernon Avenue and the chance at a better life. She must thank her auntie for keeping her involved in many activities, which helped to create her character. Melica Niccole is thankful to the many lessons and things she remembers about Mount Vernon Avenue, such as tutoring lessons, Martin Luther King Center, Coming Home, and much more. Thank you, Mount Vernon for helping to prepare many of us for the "real" world.

Unity, socialization, and community are a part of the Mount Vernon Avenue area. Things are continuously changing there, just like most things in life are changing. This change can be for the better and sometimes for the worst. It is up to the people within the community to welcome the change or to do away with what does not quite fit in their neighborhoods. I say, onward and upward Mount Vernon. Continue your legacy and make us all proud.

DISCUSSION QUESTIONS

1. Are you familiar with Mount Vernon Avenue?

2. If so, what do you remember about Mount Vernon?

3. What is your relationship with Mount Vernon Avenue and the people who live or lived there?

4. Are you originally from Columbus, Ohio? If not, where are you from?

5. Name a prominent area from your hometown or current hometown?

6. After reading Mount Vernon Avenue, what do you think each person loved or learned during their time visiting Mount Vernon Avenue?

7. Is there a similar place in Columbus, Ohio or surrounding areas similar to Mount Vernon Avenue?

8. If you can explain four experience in Mount Vernon or a similar area with one to three words, what would you say?

MOUNT VERNON HISTORY

Artwork created by Aminah Brenda Lynn Robinson
Visit http://database.aminahsworld.org/works/119

History of the Near East Side
Visit http://eastpact.org/history-of-the-near-east-side/

CSCC Library's Art Collection: Our Mt. Vernon Neighborhood
Visit http://library.cscc.edu/c.php?g=126555&p=827830

Columbus history: Highlights of our past
Visit http://www.dispatch.com/content/stories/projects/text-timeline.html

Image Collections
Visit http://digital-collections.columbuslibrary.org/cdm/search/collection/ohio/searchterm/Vernon/field/all/mode/any/conn/and/cosuppress/

King Arts Complex
Visit http://kingartscomplex.com/

Columbus Urban League
Visit http://www.cul.org/

King Lincoln District
Visit
http://kinglincolndistrict.com/dining_entertainment

Feel free to use a search engine to find other information about Mount Vernon Avenue. You can use some of the following key words: Mount Vernon Avenue and Columbus, Ohio

ABOUT THE AUTHOR

Melica was born into a one-parent household with three other siblings on the southeast side of Columbus, Ohio. Being the youngest of five girls and one brother was not always easy and she had to continuously show precision with hard work and dedication.

Writing has always been an essential part of Melica's life. It helped her creatively express certain things in her life, as well as the lives of others. Melica continues to produce material that is close to her heart and that will make a difference in the lives of others. Keep an eye out for more poetry, children's books, and much more.

Continue to follow her journey at MelicaNiccole.com.